Punctuation

AGE 9-11

Boswell Taylor

As a parent, you can play a major role in your child's education by your interest and encouragement. This book is designed to help your child learn the basic principles of punctuation. Punctuation is a code of marks which is used to make our meaning clear when we write. Confidence in punctuation will support your child's performance in all school subjects.

Each punctuation mark is explained and then there are exercises to practise each point. These are followed by a test to check your child's understanding. Answers to all the exercises and tests are given at the back of the book.

Punctuation mark	Page number
Full stop	4
Capital letters	6
Comma	8
Question mark	10
Exclamation mark	12
Quotation marks	14
Apostrophe	16
Hyphens, dashes and brackets	20
Colons and semi-colons	21

*Hodder
Children's
Books*

NCPTA

The only home learning programme supported by the NCPTA

How to help your child

- Make sure your child completes all the exercises for each punctuation mark. Practising punctuation in context is the best way to gain confidence.

- Encourage your child to check answers by reading them aloud. The punctuation should help the words flow naturally and make the meaning clear.

- If your child gets answers wrong, talk through the explanations of the relevant points to make sure they have been fully understood. Then suggest your child has another go at the exercises.

- Remember that the use of punctuation changes gradually over the years. There is a tendency now to use less punctuation than in the past.

- Concentrate on your child's successes and give plenty of praise and encouragement.

Published by Hodder Children's Books 1995

10 9 8 7 6 5 4 3

ISBN 0 340 65114 8

Printed and bound in Great Britain

Hodder Children's Books
A division of Hodder Headline plc
338 Euston Road
London NW1 3BH

Why we need punctuation

When we talk we can do all kinds of things to make our meaning clear. We can put words into groups or separate them. We can pause for breath or effect. We can emphasize words or phrases to make them sound important. We can raise our voices to indicate that we are asking a question. We can express our feelings by exclaiming with joy or surprise or fright.

We can do none of these things when we write. We therefore use a code to make our meaning clear. The code tells the reader how to read the words we have written. This code is called punctuation and the code signs are called punctuation marks. These are the code signs. These are the punctuation marks:

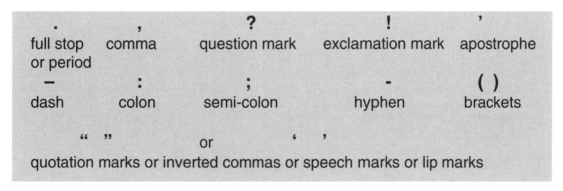

.	,	?	!	'
full stop or period	comma	question mark	exclamation mark	apostrophe
–	:	;	-	( )
dash	colon	semi-colon	hyphen	brackets

" "   or   ' '

quotation marks or inverted commas or speech marks or lip marks

You will find these punctuation marks in letters and books. You will see them on television and computer screens, and nearly everywhere that you can see words. Without written marks of punctuation to replace speech signals, we could not make our thoughts clear. Punctuation marks help the reader to understand our ideas. Punctuation marks can give a different meaning to the words in a sentence. Look at this sentence:

What are we waiting for Lisa?

This is one meaning …   **What are we waiting for, Lisa?**
Change the punctuation marks
and we have another meaning …   **What! Are we waiting for Lisa?**
Again …   **What are we waiting for?**
Lisa.

The punctuation code is essential to reading aloud. Try reading aloud what you have written, and then you will know if the punctuation has made your meaning clear.

A sentence begins with a capital and ends with a full stop

The full stop (or period) is the punctuation mark most frequently used.
A full stop is necessary when a speaker stops for breath.
It brings a statement or a single idea to an end.

Punctuate the following. Begin each sentence with a capital letter.
End each sentence with a full stop.
Note that the first one is done for you. (This rule applies to each exercise in the book.)

A 1 the cowboy was thrown from his horse
     The cowboy was thrown from his horse.

2 she climbed the mountain to its snow-capped summit

3 rockets shot into the sky

4 we are going to the fair

5 the tiger leapt upon the back of the frightened animal

6 the spacecraft landed on the moon

Six sentences have been split up. Here are their endings:
netted the floundering salmon   looped the loop
hit the ball into the air   painted a picture of the barn
reached the sunken wreck   skidded round the corner

Give the correct ending for each beginning shown below:

B 1 The impatient batsman hit the ball into the air.

2 The fisherman

3 The diver

4 The motorcyclist

5 The brave pilot

6 The artist

4

Full stops are used in some abbreviations

Abbreviations are the shortened form of words or phrases. They often consist of the initial letters of the words in the phrases.

Use full stops after initials in names. Write only the initials of the first names.

A 1 Frederick George Smith   Susan Joanne Edmunds

     F.G.Smith ....   *S.J.Edmunds* ....

  2 Write your own name in its abbreviated form.

    ....

  3 Write the abbreviated names of three people you know.

    ....

Full stops are placed after some abbreviations where the final letters of the word(s) are missing. They are also used in titles containing words that begin with both capital letters and small letters. Here are some examples:

   Nov.   ch.   Prof.   k.p.h.   v.

Write the following as abbreviations.

B 1 Department of Trade ....*D.o.T*.......   2 Bachelor of Science ....

  3 December ....   4 page ....

  5 Telephone ....   6 department ....

For what words or phrases are these the abbreviations?

C 1 k.p.h....*kilometres per hour*.............2 Nov. ....

  3 ch. ....   4 v. ....

Most abbreviations are now used without full stops, for example BBC, RSPCA, LBW. Mathematical and scientific terms are usually written without stops. Examples are kg, cm, ml.

Contractions which include the last letter of the original word do not have stops. Dr, Mr, Bros and St are examples. Can you find more?

Write the following as abbreviations without full stops:

D 1 British Broadcasting

    Corporation ....*BBC*.............2 millimetres ....

  3 Member of Parliament ....4 Justice of the Peace ....

How to use capital letters

Capital letters are used to begin sentences.

Punctuate these instructions. Write in sentences using full stops and capital letters. There are five sentences:

A ask a friend to hold a coin tightly in his or her hand inform your friend that you can tell the day's date put your hand on his or her head pretend to think hard tell your friend today's date

Ask a friend to hold a coin tightly in his or her hand.

....

....

....

....

....

Capital letters are used to begin special names.
Write names which are examples of the following:

B 1 king   president   admiral
   Arthur
   ....

  2 ship   pop group   horse
   HMS Victory
   ....

  3 country   continent   city
   France
   ....

  4 mountain   river   desert
   Snowdon
   ....

Capital letters are used for 'I' (capital 'i') and to begin words in titles.
Write titles which are examples of the following:

C 1 an adventure book *The Thirty-nine Steps* ....

  2 a computer game ....

  3 a pop song ....

  4 a poem ....

  5 a television programme ....

   ....

Capital letters are also used to begin direct speech and lines of poetry.

★ Now test yourself (capitals and full stops)

Punctuate the sentences in A and B using the capital letter and the full stop:

A 1 the dog barked when the burglar approached

   ....

   2 as he passed through the laser beam the gates shut

   ....

   3 no one knew the answer

   ....

   4 the horseman was lost in a cloud of dust

   ....

B the prized mascot of an american regiment in germany was a buffalo
   named cross-eyes they kept it in a large cage a british regiment felt sorry
   for the animal one morning the buffalo disappeared in its place was
   an oxo cube

   ....

   ....

   ....

   ....

   ....

C Write this verse in five lines adding capital letters and full stops
   where necessary:
   there was an old man of kildare, who climbed into a very high chair; then
   he said,"here i stays, till the end of my days" that immovable man of kildare

   ....

   ....

   ....

   ....

   ....

A comma marks a brief pause in a sentence

The insertion of commas can change the meaning of a sentence:

Fiona, my friend, is riding the horse. (Fiona is riding the horse.)
Fiona, my friend is riding the horse. (Fiona is not riding the horse.)

Insert the commas in these sentences to give the meaning intended:

A 1 Carpet for sale, the property of a lady, too large for her house.
  2 The man was killed while cooking the dinner in a frightful way.
  3 Wanted: piano for a man with a patterned front and mahogany legs.
  4 The clown who knew the girl wore patched trousers and had a red nose.
  5 The mother bought a comb for the baby with plastic teeth.

In this sentence the comma has been inserted *in the wrong place*.
Rewrite the sentence correctly, with two commas:

  6 The Earl who was the chieftain of his clan wore nothing, to show
    his rank.

Commas are used to separate names in a list:
**Children go to school on Monday, Tuesday, Wednesday, Thursday
and Friday.**

Answer the following questions in sentences, choosing the correct items from
each list.

B 1 Which three are birds?   wrens, robins, zebras, fawns, swifts
    Wrens, robins and swifts are birds.

  2 Which three are flowers?   roses, pearls, whelks, pinks, tulips

  3 Which three are furniture?   tables, attics, divans, anoraks, sofas

  4 Which three are fruits?   apricots, goblets, pears, tangos, plums

  5 Which three are drinks?   nectarines, milk, wagtails, coffee, tea

Commas may be used to separate a sequence of actions or instructions:
**Climb the hill, cross the river, walk along the lane and you will reach
the farm.**
We use commas to divide numbers **(5,683,542)** but not in dates **(1983)**.
In high numbers we sometimes use a space instead of a comma.

★ Now test yourself (commas)

Punctuate the following, inserting commas where necessary.

A 1 The farther he travelled the more weary he became.
   2 I will go but you will stay here.
   3 The deeper you dig however the wetter the ground becomes.
   4 Before the fire brigade arrived the house was burnt to the ground.
   5 First I would like to know which school you attend.
   6 Yes I am much better today.
   7 Jane Powell my best friend will be there to meet me.
   8 Stand in front of me Jonathan and let me take a good look at you.
   9 The prisoner wounded though he was managed to escape.
  10 There are 52678391 people living in the country.

Answer the following questions in sentences. Choose the correct items.

B 1 Which three are cities?   Manchester, Vietnam, Bonn, Oslo, Sweden

   ....

   2 Which three are games?   chess, granite, baseball, baskets, tennis

   ....

   3 Which three are insects?   ants, earwigs, weasels, eels, termites

   ....

   4 Which three are   barometers, oboes, guitars, violins, buoys
      musical instruments?

   ....

   5 Which three are minerals?   sonatas, zinc, iron, tungsten, migraines

   ....

To help you   Commas are used to help the reader, not to confuse him or her.
They indicate a pause or a change in the expression or tone of voice. Try
reading the sentences aloud (or nearly so) noting when you pause or
change your tone of voice.
There is a tendency for fewer commas to be used nowadays, but they
should always be used if they make the meaning clearer for the reader.

When to use the question mark

When we ask a question we use a special tone of voice.
When we write a question we use a question mark (?).
A question usually expects an answer.

The question mark is used only when an actual direct question is asked:

What is your name?   **When will you be able to go?**

Write answers to these questions:

A 1 When do leaves fall from trees?

Leaves fall .in the Autumn...

2 Where do rooks build their nests?

Rooks build ....

3 Why does a hedgehog have prickles?

A hedgehog has ....

4 Which animal has tusks and a trunk?

.... has tusks and a trunk.

5 How does a cricket chirp?

A cricket chirps by ....

6 What is the favourite food of the squirrel?

The favourite food ....

Write questions which could give these answers:

B 1 .What time does the bus leave?...

The bus leaves at noon.

2 ....

The kiwi lives in New Zealand.

3 ....

Paris is the capital of France.

4 ....

The disco is held on Thursday evenings.

Questions often begin with **What ... ? When ... ? Why ... ? Where ... ?
How ... ?**
Use the question mark after a single word that indicates a question.
Why?   How?   Where?   When?   What?

The question mark is used after a statement followed by a short question:

It never rains but it pours, does it?

Notice the comma before the question.

Add the short questions appropriate to the following statements.

A 1 You are not the tallest girl in the class, *are you?* ....

   2 April is not the wettest month, ...

   3 You can't grow onions in mud, ...

   4 We will not climb to the top of the mountain, ...

   5 You will try harder next time, ...

   6 It's cold outside, ...

This is the report you gave to the police after you escaped from a gang of kidnappers. Write down the actual questions you were asked.

The gang asked me my nationality. They wanted to know my name. They asked me why I was visiting the island. They wanted to know how much money I had. They asked if my parents were rich. They asked if they would pay a ransom for me.

B 1 *What is your nationality?*
    ....

   2 ....

   3 ....

   4 ....

   5 ....

   6 ....

Punctuate the following:

C 1 SON   Dad ☐ what has a black and red striped body ☐ two great eyes on stalks ☐ six hairy legs and a long proboscis ☐

     FATHER I don't know ☐ Why ☐

     SON   One has just settled on your bald patch ☐

  2 LADY   Do you charge for bread ☐

     WAITER No ☐

     LADY   Do you charge for gravy ☐

     WAITER No ☐

     LADY   May I have two slices of bread with gravy ☐ please ☐

How to use the exclamation mark

The exclamation mark (!) should be used with caution. Well selected words can often do the same job. A spatter of exclamation marks on a page will irritate a reader. If in doubt – miss out.

The exclamation mark is used to express strong or sudden feelings:
Help!   Good for you!   Oh!   That hurts!

It can be used to emphasize a command or a strong viewpoint:
Go away!   Attention!   I don't want to talk about it!

It can be used to show irony, sarcasm or amusement:
What a funny girl you are!   You are the last one to talk about envy!

Exclamation marks can follow sentences, words or phrases. It acts as a full stop, so the next word always begins with a capital letter.

Punctuate, using exclamation marks or question marks:

A 1 Oh dear are you going away
   Oh dear! Are you going away?
   ....

  2 Help it stings where is the ointment
   ....

  3 Get off the grass can't you see that it is wet
   ....

  4 Hurry up do you think you are the only person who wants to try
   ....

  5 Stop it I don't want to hear anything about it
   ....

  6 Let go what do you think you are doing I won't stop
   ....

Punctuate with one full stop, one question mark and two exclamation marks:

B   "My dog's got no nose ☐"
     "Poor dog ☐ How does he smell ☐"
     "Awful ☐ "

★ Now test yourself (question marks and exclamation marks)

Punctuate the following, inserting question marks and exclamation marks:

1 Where did you find the owl with the broken wing

....

2 Don't make me laugh

....

3 You are the most remarkable person I have ever met

....

4 Am I invited to your party Do you really want me to come

....

5 Will you come to me immediately I said immediately

....

6 Oh Why did you creep so quietly up to me You are frightening

....

7 Dear Dear Why don't you hit the nail instead of my finger

....

8 Goodness gracious me Look at the time Shouldn't we be going

....

9 Knock Knock Who's there

....

10 What are you doing That hurts

....

11 Where are you hiding Come out at once

....

12 Now Now You have forgotten

....

To help you   The question mark and the exclamation mark suggest a tone of voice. Try reading the sentences aloud. Question marks are only used when a direct question is asked. Do not over-use exclamation marks. Ration them.

How to use quotation marks

Quotation marks are sometimes single (' '), and sometimes double (" ").
They are sometimes called inverted commas, speech marks or lip marks.

Quotation marks indicate the actual (and exact) words spoken or quoted:

"The pirates will all hang," said the captain.
The captain said, "The pirates will all hang."

Notice the comma separating the actual words spoken from the rest.

Quotation marks go round each part of a direct quotation if it is broken up:

"The pirates," said the captain, "will all hang."

Notice the commas separating the actual words spoken from the rest:

," said the captain,"

Notice also that, as the quotation is a broken sentence, the second part does
not begin with a capital letter.

The quotation may consist of more than one sentence:

"The pirates will all hang," said the captain. "They are all criminals.
They have killed many sailors. They must die."

Punctuate the following using quotation marks. All the other kinds of punctuation
are given.

A 1 Oh dear! I have lost my way, said the instructor, and I don't know which
   way to go.

   "Oh dear! I have lost my way, " said the instructor, "and I don't know which
   way to go."

2 I hit the ball over the wall, said the boy, and we can't find it.

   ....

   ....

3 Stop that thief! cried the old lady.

   ....

   ....

4 Kate said firmly, I want my banana now, Grannie.

   ....

   ....

5 Ah! I recognise you now, said the shopkeeper. Aren't you the man who
   gave me a fake five pound note?

   ....

   ....

Punctuate the following using quotation marks.
The other kinds of punctuation are given.

B 1 I have lost my memory, said the patient.
      When did that happen? asked the doctor.
      When did what happen? said the patient.

  2 We have a hen, said Jackie, that lays brown eggs.
      Well, what is so wonderful about that? asked Meg.
      Could you do it? asked Jackie.

  3 A boy was swimming in a private pool. The owner saw him and was very
      annoyed. He shouted to the boy, You can't swim in this pool. It's private.
      The boy answered, I am not swimming. I am only trying to stop
      myself sinking.

These are reported conversations. Using quotation marks, write out the actual
words spoken:

C 1 Jerry asked Tom how he had got on in the milk-drinking competition.
      Tom answered that he had won by three laps.

      ....

      ....

      ....

      ....

  2 My mother said that Maggie knew that she must not eat with a knife.
      Maggie replied that she did know, but her fork leaked!

      ....

      ....

      ....

      ....

  3 Write a story of your own using quotation marks.

How to use the apostrophe 1

The apostrophe (') is used to show possession.
 John's bat = the bat that belongs to John
 Jilly's bike = the bike that belongs to Jilly

Rule One   In the singular (referring to only one owner) use the apostrophe
 + s.
Make the following possessive, using the apostrophe:

A 1 the spade of the gardener ..... *the gardener's spade* .....

 2 the cow of the farmer .....

 3 the tape-recorder of the teacher .....

 4 the ring of the bride .....

 5 the song of the thrush .....

 6 the engine of the car .....

Rule Two   In the plural (referring to more than one owner) add the
 apostrophe only *when the plural ends in ------s or -------es:*

B 1 the pencils of the boys ..... *the boys' pencils* .....

 2 the sails of the boats .....

 3 the bells of the churches .....

 4 the ears of the donkeys .....

 5 the shields of the squires .....

 6 the hats of the ladies .....

Rule Three   When the plural does not end in -s add the apostrophe +s:

C 1 the boots of the policemen ..... *the policemen's boots* .....

 2 the anoraks of the men .....

 3 the homework of the children .....

 4 the cars of the women .....

Caution   Some words showing possession *never* take an apostrophe.
They are:
 its   hers   his   ours   yours   theirs
 The snake raised its head and showed its fangs.
.....

D Write a sentence for each of the words above, similar to the example.
 Do not use an apostrophe.

Write the following sentences making use of the apostrophe to show possession. The words to be changed are shown in **bold type**:

E 1 The **coats of the ladies** were taken to the cloakroom.
   The ladies' coats were taken to the cloakroom.
   ....

  2 The books were placed on the **desk of the librarian**.
   ....

  3 The mud was solid on the **boots of the workmen**.
   ....

  4 **The head of my brother** was bruised from the blow.
   ....

  5 The burglar broke into **the house of Mr Brown**.
   ....

  6 From the display the shop evidently sold **the clothes of babies**.
   ....

  7 **The voices of women** made themselves heard.
   ....

  8 The teacher was pleased with **the interest of the parents**.
   ....

  9 The family had a **holiday of three months**.
   ....

 10 Call at **the shop of Mrs Smith** on the way back.
   ....

In the following sentences insert the correct pronouns from the list.
Do not insert apostrophes: its   hers   his   ours   yours   theirs

F 1 We like our teacher; they don't like ..*theirs*..............

  2 Your front door is red; we decided to paint .... blue.

  3 The tree sheds .... leaves in autumn.

  4 The knight returned .... sword to the scabbard.

  5 I still have my sweets; you have eaten ....

How to use the apostrophe 2

The apostrophe (') is used to show that letters have been omitted when two (or more) words have been run together to make an abbreviation:

did not   didn't   we will   we'll   shall not   shan't

Abbreviate these phrases to make one word with an apostrophe in each case:

A 1 all is ....*all's*........   2 you are ....   3 I am ....

   4 that is ....   5 there is ....   6 he is ....

   7 did not ....   8 does not ....   9 do not ....

   10 would not ....   11 have not ....12 should not ....

Abbreviate these phrases. You should omit more than one letter in each case.

B 1 you will ....*you'll*........   2 will not ....   3 shall not ....

   4 he would ....   5 she will ....   6 I would ....

   7 we have ....   8 I have ....   9 they will ....

   10 who have ....   11 I will ....12 of the clock ....

Write these words as phrases of more than one word and without apostrophes:

C 1 can't ....*can not*........   2 it's ....   3 isn't ....

   4 I'd ....   5 he'd ....   6 he'll ....

   7 we've ....   8 they'll ....   9 we'll ....

   10 she'll ....   11 won't ....12 who's ....

   13 wasn't ....   14 daren't ....15 mustn't ....

   16 you've ....   17 we're ....18 who've ....

Abbreviations such as those shown above are used in speech and dialogue. The words are usually written in full in formal and polite letters and in text books.

The *o* is used in *won't* because *wol* was the old form of *will*.
Use the apostrophe in *it's* only when it means *it is*.

Write the following sentences making use of the apostrophe as an abbreviation. The words to be changed are shown in **bold type**:

D 1 **We will** arrive at six **of the clock**.

....

2 **I am** too clever and **have not** been trapped yet.

....

3 Although **it is** time to go **I will** stay a little longer.

....

4 **All is** well with us and **that is** as it should be.

....

5 Now **we have** fallen off our bikes **they will** win.

....

6 **You will** be recognised everywhere now that **you are** famous.

....

7 **There is** nowhere **you are** welcome with that frown.

....

8 We **shall not** know the result until **you have** returned.

....

9 We **do not** want to go and we **will not** go.

....

10 I **shall not** forget the way **you have** helped me.

....

11 **I would** be delighted if **you would** keep the money.

....

12 Where **there is** a will **there is** a way.

....

13 **Do not** tell me **you have** lost your shorts.

....

19

How to use hyphens, dashes and brackets

The hyphen (-) is used to mark the division of a word at the end of a line: always divide a word only between syllables. **Al-ways** is an example.

Hyphens are used in some compound words. They separate or join the words.

Insert the hyphen in the following:

A 1 son-in-law   2 vice president   3 co operative

    4 Anglo Saxon   5 hour long   6 old fashioned

Hyphens are used in numbers between 21 and 99, and in fractions:

B 1 thirty-four   2 seventy eight   3 twenty nine

    4 two thirds   5 three quarters   6 seven eighths

Dashes — which look like these — and brackets (which look like these) are used to show an aside in a sentence or for extra information to be given. A single dash may be used before an added thought at the end of a sentence. Brackets (sometimes called parentheses) enclose information and are used in pairs.

Insert dashes — wherever necessary — in the following:

C 1 You may   although I shall be surprised if you do   enjoy this music.
   2 The 'Mary Rose'   that noble ship   sank before the eyes of the king.
   3 Jonathan Thomson   if his brother cannot come   will join us at the fair.
   4 The towels   if they are not too wet   will be used to sit on.
   5 I will try   and I will go on trying   until I succeed.
   6 The sharks were man-eaters   or so I believed.

Insert brackets (parentheses) in the following. Enclose figures and references:

D 1 I used an axe   a large one   to split the wood.
   2 The stamp   showing Queen Victoria's head   was stuck to the document.
   3 One section in the book   Chapter 2   describes the spacecraft.
   4 Can you let me have twenty-five   25   pounds?
   5 I will give you eleven   11   copies of the poem.
   6 The largest crater is about 700 miles   1100 kilometres   wide.

How to use colons and semi-colons

The colon (:) is a mark of anticipation. It starts a list or introduces a quotation.

Insert the colon in the following:

A 1 Campers must bring these items: sleeping-bags, ground-sheets and food.
2 These are capital cities Paris, Moscow, London and Vienna.
3 The City of Birmingham has a motto Forward.
4 Three motorways are closed M4, M1 and M5.
5 Three drinks are served cocoa, coffee and Coca-Cola.
6 I have three favourite teams Aston Villa, Arsenal and Norwich.

A semi-colon (;) marks a pause in a sentence. It is stronger than a comma; it is not as strong as a full stop. A semi-colon (;) may be used instead of a conjunction like 'and' or 'but'.

Insert the semi-colon in the following:

B 1 Look at the map; check the route.
2 Sean works hard Jack plays all day long.
3 The king smiled kindly at Siobhan one could see he was pleased.
4 I will read the story when I come to the end you will know why.
5 The brother was quieter he entered the world of his books.
6 At noon I left everybody had left.

Sometimes a semi-colon is used after a group of words in a sentence.
Insert the semi-colons in the following:

C 1 Sirens blared; bells rang; whistles shrieked; and people cheered.
2 The engine spluttered it stopped it started again then it stopped completely.
3 The prisoner jumped the wall he ran across the field he disappeared.

A semi-colon is used between items which contain commas.
Insert the semi-colons in the following:

D 1 The group consisted of three girls: Michelle, lead guitarist; Jane, bass guitarist; and Jacqueline, drummer.
2 Three boys were key players: Darren, striker Peter, goalkeeper and Sam, sweeper.

★ Now test yourself (capitals and full stops)

Punctuate the following. The punctuation marks you need are shown on the right. Cross out each mark as you use it. You should use these and no more:

1 MOTHER: "Don't pull faces at the bulldog." “/ ”/ ’/ ./
  SON: "But, mother, he started it!" “/ ”/ ,/ ,/ !/

2 PATIENT: What can you give me for my flat feet " " ?
  DOCTOR: What about a foot pump " " - !

3 ONLOOKER: Why are you rolling the potato patch " " ?
  GARDENER: I m trying to grow mashed potatoes " " ' .

4 DINER: What has happened to this egg " " ?
  WAITRESS: I don t know madam I only laid the table " " ' , , .

5 DINER: Do you serve ducklings here " " ?
  WAITER: We serve anybody sir Sit down " " , . !

6 STUDENT: How do you make a sausage roll " " ?
  FRIEND: That s easy Just turn it over and over " " ' ! .

7 FATHER: How do you know your teacher loves you " " ?
  GIRL: She puts kisses next to each sum I do
    There " " ! .

8 PATIENT: Doctor I feel as limp as a pair of curtains " " , .
  DOCTOR: You had better pull yourself together then " " .

9 SHOPPER: I don t like the look of that codfish It s bad " " ' ' . !
  FISHMONGER: If it s looks you want why not buy a goldfish " " ' , ?

10 VICAR: Your brother is very small isn t he " " , ' ?
  BOY: Well vicar you see he is only my half brother " " , , , . -

11 CUSTOMER: This is a second hand shop isn t it " " - , ' ?
  ASSISTANT: Yes " " .
  CUSTOMER: That s lucky Please fit one on my watch " " ' ! .

12 FRIEND: So you ve lost your dog Why don t you
    advertise " " ' . ' ?
  DOG-OWNER: Don t be silly My dog can t read " " ' ! ' .

22

13	BROTHER:	Well Kate how do you like school	" " , , ?
	SISTER:	Closed	" " !
14	GRETA:	I ve changed my mind	" " ' .
	CLARE:	Does the new mind work any better	" " ?
15	MOTHER:	Have you filled the salt cellar yet Nesta	" " , ?
	NESTA:	No mother it s so hard getting it through the holes	" " , , ' .
16	CUSTOMER:	May I try on this dress in the window	" " ?
	ASSISTANT:	I think you should use the dressing room madam	" " , .
17	JUSTIN:	Who gave you that black eye	" " ?
	KENNY:	Nobody gave it me I had to fight for it	" " ; .
18	CUSTOMER:	I d like to buy some crocodile shoes	" " ' .
	ASSISTANT:	What size does your crocodile take	" " ?
19	PASSENGER:	Those people down there look just like ants	" " .
	AIR STEWARD:	They are ants we haven t left the ground yet	" " — ' .
20	CAR DRIVER:	Sorry I ve killed your cat I ll replace it	" " ' . ' .
	OLD LADY:	But how well can you catch mice	" " ?
21	BOX OFFICE GIRL:	That s the third ticket you ve bought	" " ' ' .
	CINEMA-GOER:	I know a girl inside keeps tearing them up	" " ; .
22	MANAGER:	Why do you want to work in a bank	" " ?
	APPLICANT:	I understand there s money in it	" " ' .
23	SNAKE-CHARMER:	Careful There s a ten foot snake in that box	" " ! ' - .
	PORTER:	You can t kid me snakes don t have feet	" " ' — ' !
24	BRIDE:	Antony wake up I heard a mouse squeak	" " , ! .
	GROOM:	What do you want me to do get up and oil it	" " — ?

Story Section

These are the punctuation marks: comma (,), full stop or period (.), quotation marks or inverted commas (" " or ' '), exclamation mark (!), question mark (?), apostrophe ('), and hyphen (-).

These stories lack their punctuation signs. Insert the correct punctuation mark in each space indicated by □. You may find it helpful to read the stories aloud.

1 A woman whose family kept many pets
   looked out of her window one day when
   she heard knocking at the door□
   A boy stood there□
   □Can I help you□□she asked□
   □Not me□□he replied□□but
   there□s a rabbit on your doorstep
   and I don□t think he can reach the bell□□

2 A motorist had trouble with his car□ He called
   at a garage□A mechanic looked at the engine□
   □H□m□It□ll take about £100 to get it
   purring again□□he said□
   □Oh dear□□ exclaimed the motorist□
   □How much will it cost just to get it
   to miaow a little□□

3 Two birds perched on a tree not far from
   an airport□Suddenly a jet plane screamed across
   the sky□
   □Did you see that□□said one bird□□I□ve
   never seen a bird fly as fast as that□□
   The other bird said□□I bet you□d go as fast
   as that if your tail was on fire□□

24

4 Peter and Paul were friends☐They often played
together on their bikes☐Peter especially
liked to ride on his friend☐s shining new
bike☐One day Peter called for Paul☐
☐I☐m sorry☐Peter☐☐said his friend☐s
mother☐☐Paul can☐t come out this morning☐☐
☐Oh☐☐said Peter☐looking disappointed☐
Then he brightened up☐☐Can his new bike
come out instead☐☐he said☐

5 Joanna had just begun school and☐already☐
she thought she could read and write☐ One day
her mother saw her scribbling on some paper☐
☐What are you drawing☐☐she asked☐
☐I☐m not drawing☐☐ said Joanna
indignantly☐☐I am writing a letter to
Sara☐☐
☐But you can☐t write☐☐said her mother☐
☐That☐s all right☐☐said Joanna☐☐Sara
can☐t read☐☐

Can you explain the point of each story? You may like to draw a picture by the side of each story. There are some more stories to punctuate on the next four pages.

6 A lion and a lioness were asleep in their
cage□much to the disappointment of a boy who
was visiting the zoo with his father□The man
put a coin in the tape□recorder machine□
As the boy listened to the description of the
animal□the lion rolled over□yawned□then
stood up and roared loudly□
The boy□delighted□pointed to the still□
sleeping lioness□
He shouted□□Put another in the box□Dad□□

7 A sword□swallower was demonstrating his
skill□He swallowed some pins and nails□
□Oh□Oh□ scoffed the onlookers□□Those
aren□t swords□They□re only pins
and nails□□
□Well□you see□□said the sword□swallower□
□I□m on a diet□□

8 A young pigeon was allowed to fly out by himself
for the first time□He just managed to get home
with his feathers bedraggled□his tail
plucked□and his wings limp□
□Whatever has happened□□ asked his mother□
□It□s not my fault□□moaned the young pigeon□
□I flew down to see what game two girls were
playing□□
□What were they playing□□asked his mother□
□Badminton□□said the young pigeon□□and□
before I knew where I was□I was the
shuttle□cock□□

9 The family had been to the circus☐They all
seemed impressed by the knife☐thrower except
Timothy☐
☐I thought he was very clever☐☐said Father☐
☐He was no good at all☐☐said Timothy☐
☐I don☐t know how you can say that☐☐said
his father☐ Look at how fast and furiously
he threw those knives at the girl☐☐
☐But he missed every time☐☐exclaimed
Timothy☐

10 A competition for the biggest pumpkin was held
at a youth club☐
A notice was put on the peg board☐
☐Pumpkin Contest☐☐it said☐
☐All those interested please sign below☐☐
Among the signatures was written the name
☐Cinderella☐☐

11 A dignified gentleman☐who did not like
children☐was enjoying a quiet read in a very
silent library☐Suddenly a class of noisy
young children came in☐They were very
excited and they were very noisy☐
Finally the dignified gentleman could stand
the noise no longer☐He called the teacher to
him☐When she returned to the class she said☐
☐Will you all make less noise☐That gentleman
says that he can☐t read☐☐
☐Then he should be ashamed of himself☐☐
said one girl☐☐ I could read when I was
only five years old☐☐

12 A man was taking a stroll through the park
when a penguin suddenly appeared in front
of him□He took the penguin to the park□
keeper and said□□I□ve found this penguin□
What shall I do□□
The keeper suggested that he take the penguin to
the zoo□
The next day the park□keeper met the same man
still with the penguin□He walked up to him□
□Didn□t I tell you to take the penguin to
the zoo□□ he said□
□Yes□□ replied the man□□and that□s what
I did yesterday□I□m taking him to the cinema
today□□

13 A policeman in the park saw a duck which had
strayed from the pool□He caught it□tied
a piece of string round its neck and led it
back to the pool□
He met two boys□They stared at him amazed□
□What do you think of that□□said one boy□
□They must have run out of police dogs□□

14 A farmer decided that his horse was overfed
by people passing through the field□He placed
a notice on the gate□
□Please do not give this horse tit□bits□
Signed□The Owner□□
A few days later he was surprised to see
another notice on the gate below his own□
It read□□Please do not pay attention to
the above notice□Signed□The Horse□□

15 A teacher was telling her class the story of
Noah and his ark□They were very impressed at
the thought of all the animals going into the
ark two by two□
□What do you think they did when they were
all in the ark□□asked the teacher□
There was silence□
□All right□What do you think Noah did□□she then asked□
□Fished□□said one girl□
□What□□exclaimed a young fisherman□
□With only two worms□□

16 A lion was roaring his way across the jungle
when he saw a wild pig□He roared□
□Who is the king of the jungle□□
□You are□□squeaked the pig□
The lion went on his way and met a deer□
He roared□□Who is the king of the jungle□□
□You are□□answered the deer□
Once more the lion went on his way□
He came upon an elephant□He roared□
□Who is the king of the jungle□□
The elephant picked the lion up with his
trunk□swung him round and threw him to
the ground□The lion picked himself up□
□All right□All right□□he said□
□There□s no need to get mad because you
don□t know the answer□□

Answers

Page 4

A 2 She climbed the mountain to its snow-capped summit.

3 Rockets shot into the sky.

4 We are going to the fair.

5 The tiger leapt upon the back of the frightened animal.

6 The spacecraft landed on the moon.

B 2 The fisherman netted the floundering salmon.

3 The diver reached the sunken wreck.

4 The motorcyclist skidded round the corner.

5 The brave pilot looped the loop.

6 The artist painted a picture of the barn.

Page 5

B 2 B.Sc.   3 Dec.   4 p.   5 Tel.   6 dept.

C 2 November   3 chapter   4 versus

D 2 mm   3 MP   4 JP

Page 6

A Inform your friend that you can tell the day's date. Put your hand on his or her head.

Pretend to think hard. Tell your friend today's date.

Page 7

A 1 The dog barked when the burglar approached.

2 As he passed through the laser beam the gates shut.

3 No one knew the answer.

4 The horseman was lost in a cloud of dust.

B The prized mascot of an American regiment in Germany was a buffalo named Cross-eyes. They kept it in a large cage. A British regiment felt sorry for the animal. One morning the buffalo disappeared. In its place was an Oxo cube.

There was an old man of Kildare,/Who climbed into a very high chair; /Then he said,"Here I stays, / Till the end of my days."/That immovable man of Kildare.

Page 8

A 2 The man was killed, while cooking the dinner, in a frightful way.

3 Wanted: piano for a man, with a patterned front and mahogany legs.

4 The clown, who knew the girl, wore patched trousers and had a red nose.

5 The mother bought a comb for the baby, with plastic teeth.

6 The Earl, who was the chieftain of his clan, wore nothing to show his rank.

B 2 Roses, pinks and tulips are flowers.

3 Tables, divans and sofas are furniture.

4 Apricots, pears and plums are fruits.

5 Milk, tea and coffee are drinks.

Page 9

A 1 The farther he travelled, the more weary he became.   2 I will go, but you will stay here.   3 The deeper you dig, however, the wetter the ground becomes.   4 Before the fire brigade arrived, the house was burnt to the ground.   5 First, I would like to know which school you attend.   6 Yes, I am much better today.   7 Jane Powell, my best friend, will be there to meet me.   8 Stand in front of me, Jonathan, and let me take a good look at you.   9 The prisoner, wounded though he was, managed to escape.   10 There are 52,678,391 people living in the country.

B 1 Manchester, Bonn and Oslo are cities.   2 Chess, baseball and tennis are games.

3 Ants, earwigs and termites are insects.   4 Oboes, guitars and violins are musical instruments.

5 Zinc, iron and tungsten are minerals.

Page 10

A Accept any answers which start with a capital letter and end with a full stop.

B 2 Where does the kiwi live?   3 What is the capital of France?   4 When is the disco held?

Page 11

A 2 is it?   3 can you?   4 will we?   5 won't you?   6 isn't it?

B 2 What is your name?   3 Why are you visiting the island?   4 How much money do you have?
   5 Are your parents rich?   6 Will they pay a ransom for you?

C 1 ,,,?.?!   2 ?.?.,?

Page 12

A 2 Help, it stings! Where is the ointment?   3 Get off the grass! Can't you see that it is wet?
   4 Hurry up! Do you think you are the only person who wants to try?   5 Stop it! I don't want to
   hear anything about it!   6 Let go! What do you think you are doing? I won't stop!

B . ! ? !

Page 13

1 Where did you find the owl with the broken wing?   2 Don't make me laugh!   3 You are the most
   remarkable person I have ever met!   4 Am I invited to your party? Do you really want me to come?

5 Will you come to me immediately? I said immediately!   6 Oh! Why did you creep so quietly up to me?
   You are frightening!   7 Dear! Dear! Why don't you hit the nail instead of my finger?   8 Goodness
   gracious me! Look at the time! Shouldn't we be going?   9 Knock! Knock! Who's there?   10 What are
   you doing? That hurts!   11 Where are you hiding? Come out at once!   12 Now! Now! You have
   forgotten!

Page 14

2 "I hit the ball over the wall," said the boy, "and we can't find it."   3 "Stop that thief!" cried the old lady.

4 Kate said firmly, "I want my banana now, Grannie."   5 "Ah! I recognise you now," said the shopkeeper.
   "Aren't you the man who gave me a fake five pound note?"

Page 15

B 1 "I have lost my memory," said the patient.   "When did that happen?" asked the doctor.
      "When did what happen?" said the patient.

   2 "We have a hen," said Jackie, "that lays brown eggs." "Well, what is so wonderful about that?" asked
      Meg. "Could you do it?" asked Jackie.

   3 A boy was swimming in a private pool. The owner saw him and was very annoyed. He shouted to the
      boy, "You can't swim in this pool. It's private." The boy answered, "I am not swimming. I am only trying
      to stop myself sinking."

C 1 "Tom, how did you get on in the milk-drinking competition?" "I won by three laps."
C 2 "Maggie, you know you must not eat with a knife." "I know, but my fork leaks!"

Page 16

A 2 the farmer's cow   3 the teacher's tape-recorder   4 the bride's ring   5 the thrush's song
   6 the car's engine

B 2 the boats' sails   3 the churches' bells   4 the donkeys' ears   5 the squires' shields
   6 the ladies' hats

C 2 the men's anoraks   3 the children's homework   4 the women's cars

Page 17

E 2 the librarian's desk   3 the workmen's boots   4 My brother's head   5 Mr Brown's house
   6 babies' clothes   7 The women's voices   8 the parents' interest   9 three months' holiday
   10 Mrs Smith's shop

F 2 ours   3 its   4 his   5 yours

Page 18

A 2 you're   3 I'm   4 that's   5 there's   6 he's   7 didn't   8 doesn't   9 don't
   10 wouldn't   11 haven't   12 shouldn't

B 2 won't   3 shan't   4 he'd   5 she'll   6 I'd   7 we've   8 I've   9 they'll
   10 who've   11 I'll   12 o'clock

C 2 it is   3 is not   4 I had/I would   5 he had/he would   6 he will   7 we have   8 they will
   9 we shall   10 she will   11 will not   12 who is/has   13 was not   14 dare not   15 must not
   16 you have   17 we are   18 who have

Page 19

D 1 We'll, o'clock   2 I'm, haven't   3 it's, I'll   4 All's, that's   5 we've, they'll   6 You'll, you're
   7 There's, you're   8 shan't, you've   9 don't, won't   10 shan't, you've   11 I'd, you'd
   12 there's, there's   13 Don't, you've

Page 20

A 2 vice-president   3 co-operative   4 Anglo-Saxon   5 hour-long   6 old-fashioned

B 2 seventy-eight   3 twenty-nine   4 two-thirds   5 three-quarters   6 seven-eighths

C 1 – although I shall be surprised if you do –   2 – that noble ship –   3 – if his brother cannot come –
   4 – if they are not too wet –   5 – and I will go on trying –   6 – or so I believed.

D 1 (a large one)   2 (showing Queen Victoria's head)   3 (Chapter 2)   4 (25)
   5 (11)   6 (1100 kilometres)

Page 21

A 2 after "cities"   3 after "motto"   4 4 after "closed"   5 after "served"   6 after "teams"

B 2 after "hard"   3 after "Siobhan"   4 after "story"   5 after "quieter"   6 after first "left"

C 2 The engine spluttered; it stopped; it started again; then it stopped completely.
   3 The prisoner jumped the wall; he ran across the field; he disappeared.

D 2 Three boys were key players: Darren, striker; Peter, goalkeeper; and Sam, sweeper.

Page 22–23

2 "What can you give me for my flat feet?" "What about a foot-pump!"   3 "Why are you rolling the potato patch?" "I'm trying to grow mashed potatoes."   4 "What has happened to this egg?" "I don't know, madam, I only laid the table."   5 "Do you serve ducklings here?" "We serve anybody, sir. Sit down!"   6 "How do you make a sausage roll?" "That's easy! Just turn it over and over."   7 "How do you know your teacher loves you?" "She puts kisses next to each sum I do. There!"   8 "Doctor, I feel as limp as a pair of curtains." "You had better pull yourself together then."   9 "I don't like the look of that codfish. It's bad!" "If it's looks you want, why not buy a goldfish?"   10 "Your brother is very small, isn't he?" "Well, vicar, you see, he is only my half-brother."   11 "This is a second-hand shop, isn't it?" "Yes." "That's lucky! Please fit one on my watch."
12 "So you've lost your dog. Why don't you advertise?" "Don't be silly! My dog can't read."13 "Well, Kate, how do you like school?" "Closed!"   14 "I've changed my mind." "Does the new mind work any better?"
15 "Have you filled the salt cellar yet, Nesta?" "No, mother, it's so hard getting it through the holes."
16 "May I try on this dress in the window?" "I think you should use the dressing room, madam."
17 "Who gave you that black eye?" "Nobody gave it me; I had to fight for it."   18 "I'd like to buy some crocodile shoes." "What size does your crocodile take?"   19 "Those people down there look just like ants." "They are ants – we haven't left the ground yet."   20 "Sorry I've killed your cat. I'll replace it." "But how well can you catch mice?"   21 "That's the third ticket you've bought." "I know; a girl inside keeps tearing them up."   22 "Why do you want to work in a bank?" "I understand there's money in it."   23 "Careful! There's a ten-foot snake in that box." "You can't kid me – snakes don't have feet!"   24 "Antony, wake up! I heard a mouse squeak." "What do you want me to do – get up and oil it?"

Pages 24-29

Unfortunately, space does not permit us to include answers to the story section.